NÍNEM

Sasha Eugene

Hope you enjoy

Sasha L. Eugene.

Copyright © 2023 Sasha Eugene

All rights reserved

No part of this book may be reproduced, or stored in a retrieval system, or transmitted in any form or by any means, electronic, mechanical, photocopying, recording, or otherwise, without express written permission of the publisher.

ASIN (E-Book): B031XBQWC
ISBN (Paperback): 9798391583349
ISBN (Hard Cover):9798391583639
Independently published

Editor: Maegan Stanbury
Cover design by: Sasha Eugene

Dedication

I would like to dedicate this book to all the strong women figures in my life. We are all doing the best that we can to survive this world and without a second thought you all are willing to go out of your way to just show up. To be there. Unconditionally. The care, love, and support from the women I have met have helped shape my life story to what it is today.

Many of you watched me struggle and gave me the helping hand when needed. Many times, I turned a blind eye. Being stubborn. Not realizing then how my actions were breaking not just myself, but you women as well. I chose to learn things the hard way. I'd come crawling back more broken and hurt then before. Sometimes ten steps back from where I left off. I knew where I could go to feel safe and protected again. I knew when the lesson was learnt I had you women to go to. Each of you is a pillar in my life's story. I appreciate all the times you were there before, during, and after my mistakes. I have had the honor of having so many of you kind-hearted human beings in my life to help guide and teach me along my path.

I would like to send a special thanks to Lori Stolson! She crossed my path in the darkest of times. When weights kept being added to pin me down to the bottom of the dark ocean. She was a shining light who showed me nothing, but compassion and kindness. She is one of the most patient human beings I have met and one of the fiercest when it comes to protecting and enforcing right and wrong. You helped me to unlearn so many things that did not belong. The tools, knowledge, and insight you brought helped me to find parts of myself I thought were lost to the darkness forever.

Deb Fisher and Maegan Stanbury, I thank you from every part of my being! Throughout my school years and now "adult" life you were never shy to let your voice be heard on behalf of the students. You ensured a fair, safe, trusting school environment where I felt comfortable to share and be myself. Once I graduated you treated the kids from my home just the same. Like family. You both went beyond what your work duties called for and never faltered whether you got recognition or not. Both of you have helped my dreams and so many other dreams come true along the way.

To all you strong women, thank you! These poems I choose to share wouldn't be possible without you all.

FOREWORD

I have known Sasha since she was a child. She stayed with our family off and on as a teenager, and always will have a special place in my heart along with her son. I call her my "In and Out Girl" never staying in one place too long. That choice had its rainbows, highs, lows, and tragedy as in all rez life. We have shed many tears, many heartbreaks but also many dreams.

Sasha has always had a strong sense of responsibility and motherly instincts for her younger twin brothers and anyone else who needed some love and attention. Her door was always open to those who were just looking for a safe and stable place to call home. Always...

Putting her own needs aside as a young child. Wise beyond her years and that took a toll on her spirit. Sasha gave and gave until all I could see was a shell of who she was and could have been... It was painful to watch someone you loved being constantly hurt.

Residential School and the eternal legacy that was forced upon our Indigenous people was at the root of all issues we and many others she trusted over the years, tried to survive through. The blackness of those times and the devastation has hurt her, her family and nation to the core. Sasha cares deeply and yearns for the traditional family network, traditions, and culture. Most of all she just wants everyone to get along, be
strong, be proud, be safe and the best you can be.

Many times, I have been terrified for her life...many times. I prayed that she would find a way out of that world filled with constant turmoil and be allowed to be the person I know she was capable of, and so deserving of. Sasha is naturally highly intelligent, beautiful inside and out and a hereditary wisdom carrier. That damb "intergenerational trauma" kept hunting, haunting and finding her, her family, community, and nation at every twist and turn. I truly don't know how anyone can have that strength to keep going with the pain and the suffering she has been through. However, if anyone was to...it would be Sasha.

Sasha is a powerful, courageous indigenous woman who loves deeply. Take the time to really listen to her words and the rhythm of her life; you will learn that through the darkest of darkest times of what life was for her; one that no child or adult should have to go through, especially when survival was only held onto by a thread. Sasha holds and trusts the teachings of the Old Ones, her ancestors that stand with and behind her, and her culture continues to pull her back to the land of the living. Sasha knows that she has much to learn and share and these poems are proof she is listening and many more I can learn from them.

The Creator sent a gift along the way, the most precious gift ever...her son Jaxx. The one who gives her unconditional love, light, laughter, and the life she so deserves. She has a soft, kind, and gentle parenting way with Jaxx filled with so much wisdom...he in turn has guided Sasha back into the life worth living. The world is a better place for all of us! Love you more my girl!

Debra Fisher, 2023

CONTENTS

Nínem
Title Page
Copyright
Dedication
Foreword
Snowflakes Coming Down — 1
On These Days — 3
A Jar Of Eagle Feathers — 5
Family Photos — 11
A Familiar Memory Of Home — 12
Click Click Bang Bang — 15
I Got Time — 21
Sprinkler — 22
Where's Our Light? — 25
The Dark — 27
No Power — 29
Mirrored Image — 30
Silly Girl — 31
I Thought I Knew Pain — 34
Remain Deadly — 35
Urn body — 37
I Can Imagine — 38
Feels Like Home — 43

Hear Us	45
Moments	46
Normal Days	47
Life	48
I Was Wrong	49
Take It	50
March 10th	52
Kí7ce/Na'á	55
The Voices	59
Uncc	60
Imperfectly, Perfect	64
Hey Sis	71
Bee	72
Used To	73
Good, Bad, and Ugly	74
Spending So Much Time In Grief	76
Skoden	80
Missing You Sister	83
Reflection	86
Smudge	88
I Miss	90
I'm Sorry	91
Happy Birthday Baby Al,	94
Certificate	96
On those days	98
Fighting The Cold	107
Hastings Shuffle	108
Damn Golf Cart	109

Sperm Donor	124
A Picture Worth 1000 Words	125
Moved Back Home	132
A Great Gift	138
Want To Make It A Competition	148
Beauty in Death	151
Shell Out	152
8 Long Years	154
Glossary Secwépemctsín (Shuswap)	155
Glossary Siksiká (Blackfoot)	157
Glossary Slang	159
About The Author	161

SNOWFLAKES COMING DOWN

Snowflakes suddenly coming down
Snapping my mind out of a trance
Watching them all race
Down to the ground

Wondering which was first to fall
From the sky
Falling
To the ground

Such grace
Slowly cascading
Some spinning
Swirling

Sideways
Straight down
Some catching a breeze
And going up again

Before they really come down
Watching some get hung up
In a tree
Or stuck on the post

Others hitting that glass window
Slowly melting away
Leaving an imprint of their beauty for me to see
Before it transforms into a single tear drop shape

Subduing to gravity
Mother Nature
Gifted a new form
An old form

Using muscle memory
Rushing
Falling
To the ground

Admiration
Sitting, wishing
My falls
Were filled with such grace

ON THESE DAYS

On these days I wish I could be selfish
On these days I wish I could go back home
Even just for 5 minutes

Knowing your on your final journey home
Knowing you'll get to see everyone

My mom
My brother
My sister
Our other homies gone to soon
Far too many

Thinking of the last time I saw you
At our brothers spirit fire
At our brothers grave
Then it was us reminiscing about the good old days

Now it's just me
Crying uncontrollably
It comes in waves
Unexpectedly

Like that time you drove us all over the cliff
The tires wouldn't grip the road
The brakes went out
All of us looking at each other
You looking at me in the rear view mirror

I lit a smudge
Prayed for your journey ahead
Prayed for our journey ahead
Those of us that have to take these next steps without you

Prayed for your little baby

Prayed to my ancestors
Many you knew, asking my Mom to help ensure your transition is smooth
Prayed for you to show us a sign your okay

Today I can't control when the tears will show
Driving home
When suddenly my throat catches
And tears start to well

The pain is there
That familiar clenching
That squeezes my heart
Then radiates down my arm
And hurts my brain

On the first straight stretch
After turning on the road that leads to my home
At that corner
That you drove us over the cliff

I saw an eagle
Soaring free
Just doing circles
Free as can be
Knowing today your traveling in our valley
One of your many homes
Letting us all know
One day things will be okay

A JAR OF EAGLE FEATHERS

Seeing a jar of eagle feathers
In a house
That I'm
Cleaning

A [1]Séme7/ [2]náápiikoan home
Judging by the pictures
Memories
Hanging on the wall

Showing pride in family
Judging
Instilled in me
Hurt felt

As I didn't grow up with family pictures on the wall
Just a mantel where you will find
Individual graduation photos
And my wall leading to the basement
With many certificates of mine

From my youth
Every home growing up on the reservation
Had obituaries dedicated to one wall
Not happy family photos

Séme7/ náápiikoan shouldn't have those
Eagle feathers are
Sacred
One calls to me

To hold
I pick it up
From its spot

Nestled right beside
A pure [3]peq⁷/ [4]áápi eagle feather

Like the one I gifted my Uncc
Because at heart he was my brother
And pure like the peq⁷ eagle feather
I gifted my brother
To help on his last journey
Even though we were
Related through my séme7/ náápiikoan side
Not the [5]NDN side

[6]2S
In a new way
I see
Always said it

Always felt right
My séme7/ náápiikoan side
When explaining my family tree
Others NDN or séme7/náápiikoan puzzled

Racist??

Asking myself that too
Many times
Myself just understanding now
What I've been saying all along
Séme7/náápiikoan side
NDN side
Peq⁷/ áápi spirit
NDN spirit

2S
1 body
Realizing
Comprehending

Unc chose to try understand the NDN way

Just knowing, it felt right
For he was gifted with just being
Always helping

Always there for others
Just loving life
Lighting up a room
A warrior to the core

I used to bug him
That he was more
NDN than me
Because he was gifted a sweat

Finished a sweat
Before me
Warrior to the core
He earned it

Each of us able to unlock any gift
For we are one NRG in the end
It just depends on your capability and experience
Your willingness to put the work in to earn it

Those gifts that came from that sweat
To my brother
To Uncc
Those gifts that came from that
NDN treatment center
To my brother
My Uncc
[7]Apistotoke/ [8]Tqeltkúkwpi7
His helpers
Recognizing him
Made me so proud
Seeing what he accomplished

Who am I to say

This person didn't earn this gift
This eagle feather in my hand?
That is now speaking to me?

For I am part séme7/ náápiikoan too you see?
Do people say that about me?
Half breed title
Running through my mind

[9]Sq'wteẃs/ [10]aanáokitapiikoan
Oh I've heard it 1000 times
Both from the Caucasian
And NDN society
Filthy Half Breed
Sq'wteẃs/aanákitpiikoan

Never quite able to find my place
Wondering now
Do people say that about me?
Even though I still strive to learn the NDN way, because it feels right

Knowing choice is a gift
Choice to believe
In what we feel is right
Choice in choosing what
To do with your own NRG

With what and where we prefer
To put it
To use it
And accept it

Who are we to say
This family didn't earn this gift
Without hearing their story
And now an unknown story to this family

How picking up a sacred eagle feather in there home
Helped me to my core
Changed my own perspective
Their earned gift

Gifting me a gift
In their own home
2S in a new way
A [11]peq7/ [12]áápi one on the outside

But it's what lies within
New perspective
Changed to the core
Who is NDN society to deem

[13]Séme7/ [14]náápikoan society unworthy of these gifts
Will they deem my son unworthy
Blonde hair
Blue/grey eyes
Water fluid flowing
Change grey like a tornado
Seen in his eyes
Sacred

Sacred
Eagle feathers
Left upon this earth
By a brother
Or sister
Eagle

Eagle feather
Cascaded down
From that sacred eagles body
With the gentle loving hands
Of [15]Apistotke/[16]Tqeltkúkwpi7 blessing

To leave in just the right spot
For just right person
At just the right time
Apistotke/Tqeltkúkwpi7 himself deems appropriate

Who are we as NDN society to say Apistotke/Tqeltkúkwpi7 was wrong
Leaving a sacred eagle feather to
A séme7/ náápikoan home
Or even to an indigenous one where they are just starting to
Believe in that feeling, one NRG
The Red Road

FAMILY PHOTOS

Family photos
All taken at funerals
The numbers
Of our family dwindle
No more bushy family tree
No future roots left
No heartbeat
Passed
Passed on
To create future family
Leaving me all alone
One lonely branch
We started out such a healthy tree
We had so many branches

A FAMILIAR MEMORY OF HOME

Packing in fire wood
All 4 brothers near
Competitive
Who could carry more

[17]Kyé7e cooking in the kitchen
It smells really good
Our parents near
Competitive

How fast could we get this done
Always rushing
8 pieces of wood
My personal record that day

Competitive
Rushing, getting work done
Missed the last step, sprained bruised ankle
All 4 brothers instantly by my side

My parents, grandmother, great grandparents and sister right there
Hanging over the railing, crowding the stairs
All saying are you okay

Between the tears
Saying I will be from the heart in so many different ways
Falling, failing, hurting, crying
Being lifted, carried, mended, a sense of family; a glimpse back of how it truly used to be

Caring, care, from the heart a medicine, a way of our people
I'm really okay. No more tears in my eyes.
Laughter
Look where you're going

Chee you look reeealllyyy ugly when you cry
Better watch where you walk
You fly better on your broom
Next time you better just stay in the kitchen
Carry less

Teasing a medicine, a way of our people
Laughter
Making light of the situation
Teasing

Lessons learned for that me, at that time
Next time I'll just count the stairs
Still do, [18]tsútsllke7/[19]ihkitsik
Count every step, no matter how big or small the load I carry

Laughter a medicine, a way of our people
Food is ready
This time I'm lucky enough
Not to have to fight my way into the kitchen

My sister stops the boys from rushing
My sister brought me a plate, respect gained and given on each side
Silence as everyone takes the first few bites
Enjoying the gift on our dinner plate

Food a medicine, a way of our people
[20]Bepsi's cracking around the table
Sugar, full bellies kicking in
Praise to the cook

Praise a medicine, a way of our people
Cleaning the kitchen
Getting the work done, together
For the cook don't do dishes around here

Relaxing a medicine, a way of our people

Gathering in the living room
Happy sharing stories, a way of passing wisdom
Learning

Packing in wood
Work a medicine, a way of our people
An old
Familiar sense of home

CLICK CLICK BANG BANG

This world I was born into is cruel
The things I have seen
Endured
Survived

Its endless
Some nights
Most nights
I can't sleep

These things keep me up at night
Different thing each night
It picks at my brain; plays on a steady loop
Heck most nights the thoughts follow me into my dreams, too

Click
Click
Bang
Bang

Wanting to give it all up
Knowing I won't
But it doesn't stop the intrusive thoughts
Did I take my meds today?

Click
Click
Bang
Bang

The hopelessness of tomorrow
The hopelessness of next month
Year
Decade

Click
Click
Bang
Bang

The hopelessness for our future generations
Thinking of the battles I've overcome
Thinking I've been making things easier for them
For my son

On these late silent nights
Thinking, knowing
My generation
The generations before

Have taken in so much trauma
Inflicted by the [21]séme7
Passed on to our own red nations
There is still so much more to come

Click
Click
Bang
Bang

What happens when the last "Shuswap F1" is labeled
Only "Shuswap F2's" across our little nation
No more freedom for our next generation on who to love
Was there ever really?

Click
Click
Bang
Bang

Me
My family

NÍNEM

My ancestors
Worked so hard to care for this land

This land I can not pass on to my son
This land that has been tended to
For generations by my blood
Including my son

Click
Click
Bang
Bang

Me an F2
My son considered séme7/náápiikoan by the government
And across nations that only see that way of thinking
So much change needs to happen

Click
Click
Bang
Bang

These thoughts that keep me up at night
I wonder do others think these too
What happens when there is no more "legal NDNs"
When we've played right into their hand

How many years until the headlines read
The last F2 NDN has passed away
What happens to our bloodlines then
They won't be entitled to our lands

What will happen to Indian Affairs
The government created band offices
Will there be an uprise then?
So many séme7/náápiikoan folk out of their government jobs

Click

Click
Bang
Bang

How many years until there is only 16 Secwepemc Bands
17 Secwepemc Nations, now
Forming one of the largest indigenous populations in B.C.But how many years until there is only
15?
10?
5?
4
3
2
1
0 Secwepemc bands

Click
Click
Bang
Bang

What happens to our lands?
What happens to what little say we have now when it comes to caring for Mother Earth?
The money the government will get from the indigenous trust/lands will be astounding

No more making us run around
Providing numbers
Blood quantum
Living up to your government paperwork

Making us prove how many NDNs we have living on reserve
How many off reserve
Tell us do we qualify for funding?
Funding from our own trust money?

Click
Click
Bang
Bang

Trust that isn't all there, used to create
Ohh Canada
Ohh Canada the friendliest country
Unless you're a savage NDN

Click
Click
Bang
Bang

When their job to eliminate the savage is done
"Integrated" into proper human beings
They will get what they wanted
Complete ownership of these gifted lands

Click
Click
Bang
Bang

Did I take my meds today
Is that why I'm so discombobulated
I've tried everything
These thoughts, they won't stop

Click
Click
Bang
Bang

I wonder what our numbers are?
[22]Kenpésq't Nation
I wonder if our numbers would qualify us to be on an

endangered list?
Panda, Polar Bear, Brown Bear, Orca, Turtle, Kinbasket NDN, Bison, Kenpésq't NDN, Spix's Macaw

Click
Click
Bang
Bang

Would we make the headlines then
<u>LAST OF THE SHUSWAP</u>
Or would it just casually be thrown in
One day under the worlds other worthy news

Click
Click
Bang
Bang

Tired of fighting
Every day I've fought
To survive
28 years
And ongoing

I GOT TIME

Today isn't a "good" morning
It's a mourning
I knew it would be
I tried to keep my head up
Tried all the tools to keep my depression at bay
Today
But it is still a morning
In mourning
One where it's hard to see the good
But then
I got time
Took time
To try to understand
Why they were taken
My family
A part of me
Called back home
To [23]Apistotoke/[24]Tqeltkūkwpi7 too soon

SPRINKLER

Yesterday my boy completed a first
He was scared
And nervous
Not completely sure of himself

He didn't think that he could do it
Moving a sprinkler for the first time
Seeing his mother do it
Numerous times

Working to water this grass
Taking care of the land
That has provided for my family
For many moons

With good times
Spent with family
Provided food on our table
The income to support us

Medicine to help us
It's held us in heart shattering times
Providing us comfort
And connections

I had so much admiration
At his courage
I knew he could do it
Watching him run around in circles

Trying to catch the sprinkler head
To move it just a little closer to the dry burnt spot
Going in once but getting startled of the strong spray
Running back saying "Mommy I can't do it"

Giving encouraging words
Knowing he can do this
I watch an eagle soar in over the course
I thought of all my ancestors above

All of Jaxx's ancestors above
How I was wishing they were here to share in this
Knowing that eagle was them speaking to my son
I tell Jaxx to stop and look up in the sky

That there is an eagle soaring high
We both stop and watch as the eagle glides
Right above where we are putting the work in
I tell him see that's a sign

Even they know you can do it
That's them sending you a sign
Bringing you extra strength
You can do this

He runs in one more time
Grabs the sprinkler by the head
And moves it the few steps required
Giving the grass a drink

He asks: "Mom, is that good?"
My boy that is perfect

We get on the cart and watch the eagle circle round
One last time
As we're driving down Number 3
Before it heads back down to the river

We both say see yah later eagle
I say a little thank you
My heart feeling so many emotions inside
Grief, anger, sadness, loneliness, Pride…

For my family on the other side

Knowing, wishing you had more time to spend here on this side.
Remembering all the times this course used to be a working playground
For my mother, father, brothers, sisters, aunts, and cousins

Now it's just my boy and I out here today
But the pride for my boys first shines through
He's going off about how heavy that hose is
And the sprinkler too
I concur that it's a big job for a little man that's only been around the sun 7 times
Agreeing that he will be a pro in no time

WHERE'S OUR LIGHT?

They say I'm being selfish to want to keep you here with me.
But why does the world keep taking loved ones?
Why my mother, father, aunt, brothers, and sister;
don't you have enough Angel's?

Why do you take so much from me and my family?
Why do you have to take them so young?
Why did you have to allow something as evil as amphetamine,
methamphetamine and alcohol to be created?

It is wiping out our people
Not just the addicts, but the sober ones around them.
How much strength do you expect us to have?
How long are we supposed to battle within ourselves?

Why must you make us watch our family struggle?
How long are we supposed to go unheard?
How many times are we supposed to be brought to our knees?
With our heart exposed lying in front of us
Being expected to rise again,
and again.

Only to be kicked right back down harder and worse than before.
Still being expected to rise again with no demons attached.
Not only this, but then I must look into my little boy's eyes and
watch his innocent little world crumble around him.
Watching as he realizes that heaven is a place where his
grandma, poppa, uncles and aunts go to and never come back.

If you asked me today I would tell you that the universe is the
selfish one.
Where is our light at the end of the tunnel?
When will the endless trauma cease,
not just for me or my family, but for the people?

How many generations must be affected?
How long must we walk and live each day in this endless nightmare?
Whilst still being faced with racism, criticism and theft from the media, society and government.
When I was born into this world I was a 6th generation.
That makes my son a 7th generation.

Today I no longer can see any form of light at the end of the tunnel.
Rest in peace sweet sweet sister Bee.
Just because I can not see the light at this moment.
That doesn't mean I'm going to stop looking.

No matter how hopeless and lifeless I myself feel.
For my family is my everything .
I will do anything I can to make life easier on the living generations and our future generations.
To make all my angel's proud.
Even if it starts with a couple of gems.

THE DARK

Some days the dark
Just calls my being
Some days
Sometimes
Turn into a week
Some weeks turn into two
Sometimes weeks
Turn into a month
Sometimes a month has turned to months
Alone in the dark

Love having to be forced
When I really just want to stay in bed
Not eating
Not sleeping
Sometimes
Eating way too much
And sleeping way too much

I'm tired
Not just my body
Not just my brain
But my soul to
How much is too much
How can I go on
Especially whilst losing hope of love

Always wanting to cry
Always feeling so angry
Always feeling the dark
The dark trying to take over
Those days
Weeks

Months
I fight

I Fight
My brain
My body
My soul
Trying to remembering the love
Through it all
Trying to focus on what I have to be thankful for

NO POWER

What the eff happened to my power
Stollen
Taken
Givin
Battery low
Sittin in a dark quite house
Lost
Beaten
Betrayed
It's so quiet I can hear the clocks
Ticking from down the hall
Thank [25]Apistotoke/[26]Tqeltwkúkwpi7
That ticking
Pulled me outta the dark
Tick
Tock
Tick
Drowned out the dark intrusive thoughts
Tock
Tick
Tock
Overthrew all the voices rattling off in my brain

MIRRORED IMAGE

Getting ready for the day
Facing the biggest obstacle
Myself in the mirror
Prepping my skin for the day
Putting those warrior marks on
With plain old lotion
Laughter
Power
That will soak into my skin
Protecting it
Silently
Throughout the day
Coating my face in an invisible mask
Protecting it
From the worst
Me
My spiteful self

SILLY GIRL

What is wrong with me
They should be right there
They are mine
Mine alone
Reach left
They scuddle right
Reach right
They prance left

.

..

...

SURPRIZE ATTACK

...

..

.

They don't flinch

.

..

...

I beg
Please just give them back
I survived everyday
I didn't give up
I'm not giving up
They are mine

.

..

...

DEAD AIR

...

..

.

PLEASE GIVE THEM BACK

.

..

...

Something breaks silence to declare:
?????: "My dear, your memories are eschewed."

.

..

...

But why?
Why do I deserve this?
Who are you to say this?
...

..

.

????: "Humor me and lend me your ear child. Tune into me and you will know. They are not yours but ours, I've kept them inaccessible for our well-being."

.

..

...

"But I NEED them, that's all I got left of my childhood and my family. They are all gone. WHO ARE YOU?"

...

..

.

????: " Give me credence, silly girl. We can't handle it all at once. I will keep them safe until it won't cripple us."

.

..

...

"Noo please, I want to remember NOW!"

...

..

Soul: "[27]Kitatama'sino"

I THOUGHT I KNEW PAIN

I thought I knew pain 20 years ago...
But she was still uncharted.
I thought I was conversant with pain 15 years ago...
But she was still an alien.
I thought I tussled with pain 10 years ago...
But she was still eclipsed in darkness.
I thought I was acquainted with pain 5 years ago...
But she was still foreign and unmapped.
I thought I was familiarized with pain 3 years ago...
But she was just doing her surveillance.
I thought I opened up to pain 2 years ago...
But she did not divulge destiny's plan.
I thought we had come to harmony 1 year ago...
But she invaded, annihilating any notion I had of her.
I thought I could coincide with pain...
But she is malevolent in testing my resolve.
I thought she would never leave...
But after months she did.
I thought I could subsist through the carnage and massacre...
But she had different machinations.
I thought I was making strides...
But she caught me by surprise.
I thought I could fracas with pain...
But she was stronger, she left me on the ground ebbing away.
I thought I knew pain...
But she is just a beautiful unruly stranger.

REMAIN DEADLY

The body remembers
Teaching my body
It's okay
We don't have to be in survival

We can thrive
Yesterday was a hard day
I was crashing
I did crash

I am only one being
Too many tears
For hours
Letting it flow
Letting it go

Taking it to the mountains
Lucky enough to be surrounded
By such sacred strength
All around

Many spirits
Blessed
For even grandfather mountain
Crumbles
Shakes
And roars

Letting the world know
When he has too much to hold
Letting go
Of the boulders
Stones
Trees

The extra weight
That is too heavy to hold
That no longer serves
His slow growing process

I will rise
I am rising
Slowly
Standing

Remaining strong
Solid
Deadly
Like our grandfather
The mountain

URN BODY

My unconscious self
My unconscious mind
Is when I'm wide awake

Never able to rest
Even when my physical body does

Maybe that's why I can't sleep, too afraid
That this might be good bye to this self

Lost to the night

The one urn I have slowly grown to love
Scared I won't make it back to this vessel

From wherever it is I must go
When I'm wide awake

When others are wide awake
Scared I won't want to fly back from that place

Where all we know is love
Where all we give is love

No repercussions
Just teaching, learning, awakening

One energy
Love
Cleansing
The soul

I CAN IMAGINE

I can imagine a time whilst I sit here beading
A time way back when
When we were all one
The medicine wheel I'm creating reminding me
Of all its teachings
Many are held within
This one circle

The circle of life
Creation
How it should be
How it was
Once upon a time way back when

I can imagine a time when this
Just sitting and beading would be enough
My only obligation for the day

I can imagine a time where these summer breaks were our life
Rising with grandfather sun
Enjoying all his warm long days has to offer
With family by your side

The first summer I'm not stuck working like a bee
To just barely survive
Not worrying
Things will work themselves out

I can imagine a time where the foreign language was still english
A time when our [28]Kyé7es and [29]Slé7es were trying to teach us this new tongue
So many of us not being able to understand [30]Secwépemctsín
It's almost a lost dialogue
Oh how it's backwards now

Only 200 years ago we would communicate in our own tongue
Speaking it freely on a daily basis
How it should be
How it was once upon a time way back when
Secwépmec/Siksiká strong

I can imagine a time when our children got to stay with us all day
Our nation's children outside playing together
Watching us
Listening to us
Learning from us
Whilst we get work done
Staying with family
Staying with a loving community
Learning our traditions
How it should be
How it was once upon a time way back when
When we were comfortable in our own ways
Secwépmec/Siksiká strong

I can imagine a time where love, kindness and respect were still honored
I can imagine a time where the [31]séme7/[32]náápiikoan still listened
To new to the land, Mother Nature
Unsure so they respected our teachings to take care of her

I can imagine a time when a human being was respected for how much they gave
Gave back to family
Give back to community
Gave back to the nation
Gave back to creation
Ohhh how I could imagine
A world untouched by the settler's hands

I could imagine the unease of our [33]teqwétsten/[34] iihtsíístapipaitapiiyo'p
Facing a new alien nation
It's not peachy trying to leave the reservation today
I could imagine back then
The hurt
The betrayal
The heartbreak
Of the Red Nations

I know the hurt of watching mother earth be destroyed
I know the hurt of watching our people slowly be taken out
I know the hurt of watching people claim "ownership" of everything
I could only imagine these same battles you went through
Once upon a time way back when
Now we face it within our own nations too

When they weren't as sneaky
Trying to wipe out the savages
Todays approach to Eradicate
Eradicate the NDN, more "humane"

I can imagine a time when
An indigenous just was
They did not have to prove blood quantum
We just were

I could imagine being content happy
Then having it torn away
I've had it happen
Just in a different time, in a different way

I could imagine watching our Red Nations get labeled as savages
We still are
I could imagine being deemed unworthy of our way of life
We still are

NÍNEM

I could imagine the silence across our camps
After our children were stolen to the horrid
Extermination camps

We are still fighting to keep our children
Just in a different way
They created "legal" systems
To watch over and intervene with our offspring
Their "legal" systems
Ready to hammer us down
Their "legal" systems
Their rules
Where they always seem to win

I could imagine our grandmothers
Mothers
Sisters
Aunts
Crys longing for their babies
Feeling helpless
I could imagine the grandfathers
Fathers
Brothers
Uncles
Battle cries
Anger coming out
Knowing fighting is useless
Their defeat hanging thickening the air
Feeling helplessness all around

I can imagine not having that powerful medicine to help lift you up
The power of the children's laughter
The power of that next generation
The power of the magic that is simply youth

I could imagine a time when our nations were not packed full of

trauma
I could imagine a time where intergenerational trauma wasn't being passed down to the next generation
I could imagine a time when my life wouldn't have had so much hurt
At 27 cycles around grandfather sun

I could imagine a time where these [35]séme7/[36]náápiikoan medical professionals wouldn't say:

I couldn't even imagine
I couldn't even imagine that's so far away from normal
I couldn't even imagine your life story you should probably write a book
I couldn't even imagine how you made it through
I couldn't even imagine growing up in that everyday life
I couldn't even imagine seeing what you saw every day
I couldn't even imagine the battles you have yet to come
I couldn't even imagine that's unbelievable
I couldn't even imagine that's what you were taught
I couldn't even imagine the levels of trauma
I couldn't even imagine all your ptsd
I couldn't even imagine the steps you've taken
I couldn't even imagine walking a mile in your shoes
I couldn't even imagine the stories from those death camps
I couldn't even imagine fighting for whom you are
I couldn't even imagine fighting the "legal" systems
I couldn't even imagine your perseverance
To ensure the future NDN is not wiped out

FEELS LIKE HOME

The days that seem impossible and nights unbearable.
Waking into the day scared and scarred.
Nightmares of my [37]kwséltkten/ [38]níkso'kowaiksi

MELANCHOLY
.

Mother?
..

Father??
...

Sister???
....

Brothers????
.....

Anybody?????
......

Auntie?? Grandma??? Grandpa????Uncle?????
....

Destroyed.Ended.Dust.Extinct
....

Awake.Existence.Memories.Omnipresent.
....

Take me demons....back to your realm.
Let me settle back and rest a minute.
I can see them on stage. It feels like home.
Orchestrate your worst.
....

For it is better than reality!
Where they will linger inaccessible in the darkness of the past.

HEAR US

Today you are remembered
Your kind soul
Your wise words
Your huge heart will not go forgotten
I pray that you help guide and lift up the lucky ones that had the honor of calling you our family/friend today
Hear our prayers
Help steer us on the path we must walk without you
Give those a little push of encouragement from above when you see them falter
Grant them a little sign to let them know you're still listening
Help renew their strength
Fly high with the eagles, until you reach the ancestors
[39]Kitatama'sino
[40]Me7 wíktsen

MOMENTS

There are some moments I capture that take my breath away
Moments that are so heavenly
I know my family sent it
To steady my soul
The creator took my family to soon
How lucky you all must be to have views like this all the time

NORMAL DAYS

Mom,
Unconsciously our memories get tucked away in a hidden room
My soul just wants to give my mind and body a break from the pain
I know my "normal" days are numbered
Before reality comes exploding from the room
Causing me to collapse gasping for air

LIFE

Mom,
It doesn't feel right that I am here and you are not
My heart beat began as I emplanted my roots into you
Your breaths gave me oxygen and your heart gave me life
From the start we were one and now you are gone
Without you I don't know how my soul is supposed to go on

I WAS WRONG

Mom,
I thought I knew what loneliness was, but boy was I wrong
Losing you has caused a ripple that just goes on
I pray for things to get easier with each passing day
But reality continues to lead us all astray
All I hear is for these twins we must pray
The hole you left will never be filled
Until that day my heart, too is still

TAKE IT

These last 3 months have felt like an eternity
Time has never moved so slow
I just want to hear you say my name
I still don't understand why you had to go

Mom, life still hasn't gotten any better
Without you here I'm not sure it ever will
My heart still aches uncontrollably
We never had much but you were always giving

I tried never to be ungrateful, but please Mom
I'm begging you to take it
Take this heartache and pain away
I swear some days I can feel you here

But honestly that is my biggest fear
Because you will never be able to stay near
Please mom stop my tears
My heart is tired and sore

Some days it's hard to go on
Then I think of our 23 years worth of memories
The smiles we once had make it a little easier
I don't know how I'm supposed to handle 23 more years without you

I could barely handle turning 24
I feel like I've failed you by being angry and sad
A wise woman once said: "There is no right way or wrong way to grieve"
I know I'll never be able to get over losing you

I promise I will get through it
I write to you almost every day Mom

NÍNEM

I hope you get my letters in the Sky World.
I love you so much Mom
I miss you so much more

MARCH 10TH

Snap tells me
March 10, 2017
5 years ago
We were just being
Being family
Grandmother
Mother
Grandson
Laughing
Jamming
Dancing
The physical memories
Heart warming
And soul shattering
How
All at the same time
Riding the up
Watching the Series
Of short videos
Memories
X2
So Jaxx could see you
Know you were there
Get a peak of seeing your personality
Remembering the warmth
Your perfume
That moment
Moments
With you
You with Jaxx
A small part of our family
In these videos

A time just for us 3
Smiling
Being
Enjoying life
Taking a moment
Family
Making each other laugh
With legit silly faces
The down
For every up
There is a down
It's those that surround you
That make
Everything worthwhile
Family
Being able to give love
And receive it
Sharing space
Visiting
Calling
Messaging
In being
In the same room
Knowing
Feeling
Still
Letting it go
Letting it flow
Of you
And the rest of the family
My stars, ancestors
Up above
I love you all and miss you so much more
Until we meet again
In that place
Filled with nothing but

Light and love
[41]Kitatama'sino/[42]me7 wíktsen

KÍ7CE/NA'Á

Today doesn't seem any easier
I really thought it would
My body feels like it's in shock
I wanna cry, but it won't come out

[43]Kí7ce/Na'á today was your day
Once a day full of only pride
Another Eugene born
The legacy goes on

We should have been celebrating
45 years around the sun
Here on Mother Earth
But now your spirit has moved on

Kí7ce/[44]Na'á I miss you
What I wouldn't do to go back in time
I'd choose your birthday
22 years ago

I'd get to spend all day with family
All of us gathered in one place
Having a day filled with extra love
A day just to recognize you

22 years ago
Auntie Amy would have still been here too
Our family would have been complete
There wouldn't be an empty seat at our table

This is your 4th birthday
I will be spending without you
This will be 19 years
Since Auntie Amy got called home

How In my heart
It only feels like yesterday that you both were here
4 years how could it be
19 years...
No way...

[double checks math with calculator]
[2022-2003= 19]
[triple checks math with fingers again]
[2019/1 finger; 2020/2 fingers; 2021/3 fingers ; 2022/4 fingers]

If only it were 22 years ago
You'd all still be here
Today wouldn't feel so heavy, like the world was crushing my shoulders
There wouldn't be a permanent vile emotional smear on this day

I'd get to give you another hug
I'd get embrace your aura
I'd get to hear your voice
I'd get to watch your eyes light up
I'd get to view your laugh catch on, until the whole room was laughing with you
I'd get to feel your love being passed on
I'd get to witness your passion for life again

Born a sister, daughter, granddaughter
Given the name Stephanie "Babes" Felicity Eugene
17 years later
You gained the name Kí7ce/[45]Niksíssta

Mom I hope you know your legacy lives on
I speak your name often
How can I not
You were such a big part of my life

You live on

I tell your grandson how much you spoiled him
I tell your grandson how often you came to visit him
I tell your grandson of the things you taught me
I tell your grandson stories of the silly things you would do
I tell your grandson about our adventures
I tell your grandson how much you loved him
I tell your grandson you watch over him from the sky world

Kí7ce/Na'á
I feel the tears coming now
The lump in my throat is moving
Pushing up into my brain, the water works are out

Kí7ce/Na'á
Auntie Amy
Two strong indigenous women
Two beautiful souls

Your bodies couldn't handle your spirits
Pitiful simple flesh
No way it could ever contain all that you were
This world was too cruel for your gentle beings
Creator called you home again
Back to that place filled with nothing but love
Until it's time to begin another life cycle

I just hope there's time for you all to wait
Until we are all there
When creator decides to call us home
I hope after that call the rest of us on this side, run on NDN time

I hope the universe allows our family to meet up in the stars again
One more family meeting
Before saying again,
[46]Kitatama'sino/ [47]me7 wíktsen

A star family
Powerful, ancient, everlasting
All this love
Moving

Nowhere to go
Feeling it all
Letting it go
Letting it flow

THE VOICES

The voices
They want me to keep going
I usually do
No rest for the wicked
You have all the time to sleep when your dead
Always others
Burnt out
Don't make me burn them
This year I promised me
Let's make this healthy
I'll take notes, little snippets
I'll dedicate a day to you
To allow myself to become a part of the gifts you bestow onto me

UNCC

Unc
One year today
My boy asking
Was it a taco Tuesday too
That day
Unc got called home
To heaven
My grief
Then putting that aside
To help with
My boy's grief
Finally able
To let it show

Unc
My brother
At heart
Unc
Unc
Unc
Unc
Unc just a title
He was there for me
As a brother should be

I covered him with a blanket
I gave him
A [48]peq7/[49]áápi eagle feather
You see
Part of a braid
What I had left
Already cut short

Already had given
Left with the rest of our family
Doing what I can
To help get his spirit
Home
As taught
In our ways
Even though
He was from my [50]séme7/[51]náápiikoan side
He was my brother at heart
Today I'm mourning

Morning the loss of a brother
Part of my hearts home
Another piece
Gone
To the sky world
Pieces of me
Left at the gates
Sent with them
With each and every single one

One year
Completed
Surviving
In
Mourning
Getting through
Each morning
His song
C'est La Vie
Gifted to me
That dreadful
Mourning

Remembering

That
Call
The one I myself
Have had to make
Too many times
Creating that
Chain of heartbreak

Change
Change that runs so deep
I still haven't been able
To unlock the words to describe it
Not sure I want to
Words carry power
Parts of feelings
Maybe just meant
For me

Feels like just yesterday
But feeling like an eternity
As I look back
And sit with these
Oh so hurtful
Soul shattering
Feelings
Unc buried
His name
Gifted
Written on a rock
That name
Wasn't all he was
That does not sum
Up
Unc
Too me

My words

NÍNEM

Gone today
My heart busy traveling
Feeling
I can barely see my screen
Through the tears
Oh how they haven't stopped
Since my eyes opened
In my dreams is where I wish to be
Maybe I'd be lucky enough to unlock a loving one of my family
For I feel them
All
The
Time
But like my boy said
I just want to see them
But he said see them physically

IMPERFECTLY, PERFECT

New me
Reborn
Feeling alone
Alone

Lost in my mind
Already writing
Finding that me time
In the morning

Taking a bit too long
Thinking of my mom
Thinking Bee & being
Thinking of different ways
Being is all around me

Old and new
Sister Bee
Just being
All around me

Instilled
Within me
New teaching
Thinking of my Mom

Knowing others are thinking
Of their own too
In the mornings
Mourning

Mom
My Mother Dearest
Taking her time

Me ready already

Urging
Let's go
Her
Getting both wings ready

To keep her steady
Getting ready for the day
Singing her sweet song
To Dad
To my Brothers
To my Sisters
To me
To herself
To the family
Creating herself
Creating that NRG
Sending up unknown prayers

Oh how she
Is instilled in me
Seeing
Old medicine
Medicines
My new medicine
Medicines
New me

Reborn
Powerful
Remembering
Moon water

Felt ready
Many different things
Power new moon
Power full moon

Power half moon
Power dark moon
Power with the sun
Power
In cycles
Power in
The rise
And fall

Power
In
Changing
Just accepting
To just be

Silencing the voice
In my mind
And around me
New medicine

Seeing
Feeling
It
Gifted to me

Many things
Now I see
Sitting in my car
Sitting listening

Smoking
Steadying
Alone
Sacred time

Coffee
Old song
Rereading the lyrics

New meaning

Feeling the beat
The NRG
Taking my minute

To just be
As it should be
As it was meant to be

Remembering
An old profile photo
Comes to thought
An old quote

Instilled
Then
New me
Searching

Scrolling
The album profile photos
Staring
At old me's

In the eyes
Right in the face
I've heard power
Lies in the eyes

Many times
Looking
Me in the eyes
Until I find the one

I chose to speak to me
For this time
I'm seeing everything
In my own eyes

Powerful
Rereading
The quote on the old profile photo
"The word "Imperfect" actually spells "Im perfect." Because everyone is perfect in their own Imperfect ways."

Didn't think to write down the author
No credit given
To him
Or to that me
At that time

Maybe I couldn't see
The mark I left on that page
Or those around me
Not knowing my singing
Alone
In the car
Was sending up
Unknown
Prayers with the
NRG

At that time
Making room for that new mark
Created
Alone
Or
Together

A new me
Staring back at me
In this rear view mirror
I used to fear

For many different
Reasons

But mostly for
The reflection
I saw staring
Back at
Me

Knowing now
That one small space
And recognition
Is powerful

Im perfect
To
Imperfect
Us as we should be

Just one
Small simple
Space

A new me
A new meaning
A new found recognition

In one small
Sacred space
Learning
With the help of others
Learning

All types of recognition
Giving credit where it's due
It's important

In others
And
Within you
Learning the power

In a
Simple
Powerful
Space

And in simply being
And believing
In your wings
And your being

HEY SIS

Hey Sis
Missing you and the silly things you would do
My photo memories tell me today 5 years ago you lived with me
You stole my phone to take pictures
Then you did my makeup, giving me wings like you
I love you and I miss you so much more
Love you long time until we meet again in that place filled with light and love
Wishing I got a material piece of your belongings
I look at the shirt you are wearing in the picture
It was one of your favorites
I see your onesie in the background
I'm brought back to all of our dance parties and chill nights
A material piece of your belongings
Something small
I know many others were hoping to get that too
That's our way
The NDN way
But our memories and laughter will forever stay
That love you shared is strong
Just wishing
For a small piece of comfort
Like that Wonder Woman shirt brought you
When times got too hard
Thankful for these pictures that pop up along the way

BEE

Today I woke up okay
Now I miss you horribly
You had just walked into my dream
When I had to wake up and start life today
I barely got to say [52]weytk/[53]oki
I keep hearing you laugh and picturing your smile
I'm trying to clean and do laundry
Our song came on
That one I would blast for you
Best Friend
When you were missing our Momma Duck
I can't help but remember all of our dance/sing offs
When we would spend more time messing around then cleaning.
I love you
And I miss you so much more

USED TO

Bee
I'm missing you
My Beautiful sister
You got this lifestyle
The hurt it took to change it
You used to call me protégé for a short time
Introduced me to many new brothers
Mourning so many
Parts of me
Others
Old lives
Dead
And
Alive
When this hurt would come
Your the one I used to talk too

GOOD, BAD, AND UGLY

Bee
Linda
Bubble butt
Duh
Bell
Bella
[54]Custwést
Auntie
Sister
Belinda Dawn

Today marks [55]seséle/[56]naato'ka years
Since you got called home

Today is another day where I can't stop the tears
Today is another day where I feel alone

I think of you every day
The good
The bad
And the ugly times

Living at this home
Having constant reminders
Ones I used to fear
To scared to let anymore hurt in

At the time I couldn't handle any more
Now having these constant reminders
I see them as a blessing in disguise
Knowing they are

NÍNEM

Remembering
The stories
The short time
We got to spend together

SPENDING SO MUCH TIME IN GRIEF

Spending so much time in grief
After loosing
Too many family
Too many friends

I really start to wonder
What the moments will be like
In my final hours
Before it is finally my time to get called home

Wondering if I will make it till I'm old and grey
Knowing I'm sober and don't live a life that could cause me to go missing
[57]MMIW sits close to home
Or will tragedy strike
Leaving everyone saying she was too young

In the seconds that feel like minutes
And minutes that feel like hours
What will it be like on this side
When it's finally my time to get called home

Please don't let there be to much bickering
And I know there will be
It's enviable
Just at the end remember the love

Be decent human beings after
And both apologize
Hug it out
Say I love you out loud

NÍNEM

For you never know when it will be your last time
Take it from someone that knows
Life can end to quickly leaving a gaping hole
Leaving you wishing those last words would've been

Love yah

My sister and I we were sitting, smoking, talking about grief
She was hurt as she was told, smarten up
Or you'll end up like your mother.
Addicted, dead, too young

Momma was such a good human being
Underneath all that pain, trauma and addiction
Always kind and caring
What he didn't know is we still looked up to her mother

But she said I'll always be here
I said duh you better be I will, too
We hugged it out
Wiped our tears

She said jokingly
I can't go
I'm not wise enough to be an ancestor
I'm not old enough to be an ancestor
Leaving us laughing

But creator decided that you were
That your journey on this side was done
Mission accomplished
Back to the stars to await
The rest of our star family

When my missions accomplished
Light that spirit fire
Feed me like the Sasquatch I was

Talk, laugh, cry, yell, scream, sing, jamm out
But just remember the love

Take the scenic route on my final trip
Throw that war pony in 4X4
Like I normally would when driving around
Take me through our nation
On those bumpy dusty rough back roads

Take me on that Eagle Ranch Road
Go slow take in the forest
The smell of dust mixing with the pine trees
I can feel the little grains on my tongue, tasting the land

So many firsts
Down that Eagle Ranch Road
My first time
Being a bomb fire host
My first buck
Dropped like a sack of nails
My first
Non-family job doing turf care
My first time
Teaching my boy to shoot a bb gun
My first
Favorite spot to sit

Remember all the times we went for a rip
Take me to one of my favorite spots
For swimming and fishing
The river
The steel bridge

Remember that time I dove with my rod and caught a fish
Sit with me in the bed of that box
Sing me home

NÍNEM

Please don't leave me alone in that war pony's box
Know I'm just as scared to go on without you
Know we are both taking new steps
I hope I'll have gained enough knowledge to be a good ancestor for you all

Even though you won't see me
I will be there
For sure on those rainy thundery days
Those were my favorite

Sitting watching the storm roll in across the prairies
Being able to see the rain coming for miles
Or watching the dark clouds creep in over the mountain tops
The thunder seems 10x louder in the mountains
Natural bass all around
As a [58]2S, Its okay for it to be woman or man
To do the job of bringing me home
We have lost to many
And our woman of our nations are some of the strongest I have had the pleasure of knowing

SKODEN

Ohh Bee
I just finished crying
Praying
For you
For me
For family
For easy healing
For our physical bond
That can no longer be
The same as it once was

Letting it go
Grieving
But I'm grateful
To be blessed with
Another memory

More tears
How are they still coming
How are there any left
I knew these
Flood gates
Would be opening

Grieving
Too many
At once
Such a short span

Yours
Really
Finally
Hitting

NÍNEM

Home
Coming out

Tears
Love never given
So much
Pouring out
Skoden

I'll straighten my crown
And if any of em effer's mess around
They will find out
Just how deadly
This Harriet Samsquanch can be

We'll dance them outside
Just like we used to do
Love you to the moon and back
Love you long time
To infinity and beyond
I know you got my back

I got yours
Feeling each other
From different sides
Of the universe
Your love was strong
My love is strong

With these strings
Attached
To you
And others I now must call ancestors
Our love is even stronger

Let them eff around and find out
I love you my sister
I miss you even more

[60]Kitatama'sino/[61]me7 wíktsen
Until we meet again

MISSING YOU SISTER

Missing you
Sister
Driving passed the graveyard
Then Mom's spot

Hearing you say
Jokingly
Creating laughter
Your smile bright

I'm not wise enough to be an ancestor
Oh how you were
In my eyes
Wise
Knowledgeable
My sister

Your protégé
In our young days
Seems like life times ago
When I think of
The days
In Siksiká
In the trailer
In the grandparents basement
When the fam
Was whole
4 brothers
1 sister

Feeling you more
Around
Feeling it
Letting it go

Letting it flow
Feeling the hurt

The loss
Missing you
Knowing you're really on the other side
Tears start pouring

Trying to stop them
Taken by surprise
I'm driving
Feeling so broken

Then seeing you soar right above the road in front of me
As an eagle
So low just circling above
The road in front of where I'm going

I know your with me
I know your there
I just wish we could
Hang out
Share
Space
Talk
Like we used to

I miss you walking in my door
I miss your hugs when my heart is broke
For many different reasons
I miss your physical support
We were warriors

You were a warrior
You helped me through so much
Even though
We both were hurting

NÍNEM

I wish I would've accepted
Your offers to hang out near the end
I know now you understand
Why

Even then
Protecting my heart
Jaxx's heart
From addiction

But it still broke
In the end
It always does
I'm sorry
I wish I saw you more
Was there for you like a true sister
In the end
I hope you know just how much you were loved

REFLECTION

Recently I was told to look at my reflection
I did
I don't know why
What was there to look at?

Today a brother from another nation
Stopped to give me his band's flag
He said he could feel power and strength
So he pulled to the side

Many others have said this before
That they could feel my power and strength too
I never really believed
Always my worst bug bear

I couldn't be more honored
My own leadership wouldn't support me
Even with a flag, twice
It made me feel unbecoming

Not just because of the flag
But personal reasons as well
I have felt this way for many of years
Made to feel undeserving of many things

Happiness, safety, comfort, boundaries
Today I let it all go
All those projections placed upon me
And those from others

I finally felt that power
I see my own strength
It wasn't the trauma that made me
I'm the one who overcame

If someone else can feel it
Why can't I?
I cried
I let it out

Please take these things not intended for me
Send them somewhere
Where they won't harm
Anyone, anything, or creation

SMUDGE

With [62]Kyé7e and [63]Slé7e
On Jan 18th
Feelings are heavy all around
It hurts to hear Kyé7e feels unworthy

Too much hurt given
And taken
Not enough healing
Forgiveness

Silent prayers
Watching the smoke rise
Doing the house
Do that fire room, especially

Being called out behind me
Lots of problems
Start there
Sitting in there

The computer room
Taking my time
Thinking of my late brother
Praying for him and his journey

The smudge just won't go out
Sitting at the table waiting
Patience
The coals keep relighting
Sending up almost smoke signals
Stoping
Going
Not finished yet

Dumping the ashes
Some fall like usual
Some take off and dance into the sky being carried towards
Top hill

Coming in
Wrapping up
The dream catcher starts swinging
Uncontrollably

Me pointing
It out
Nothing touched it
Slé7e pointing it out

Kyé7e: "Isn't that something"
Silence
As we sit
And watch it
Swing for a bit
Until it steadies

I MISS

Today it feels real
Snapped back into real life
The hurt came uncontrollably
How can this be

I miss all those years you lived with me
Where I took seeing your face everyday for granted
I miss the feeling of having your presents in the house
I miss cooking and cleaning with you

I miss our conversations about aliens
Parabolic microphones, and everything in between
I miss your smile and your big heart
I miss hearing your laugh

I miss being able to stop over and visit with you
After you had moved out
I miss your gentle spirit
Your kind heart
Most of all I just miss my baby brother

I'M SORRY

My baby brother, I miss you so.
I'm sorry I failed you.
For this I can't seem to let you go.
How can I become worthy of your forgiveness?
I let the wrong people in.
They stabbed me in the back.
You seen them as role models.
I thought they couldn't take any more.
I thought I was in the clear.
Then they stabbed you in the back.

Avulsing my heart in front of my eyes!
I wasn't always the best example.
I could have, should have helped you more.
I had to battle my own demons.
I lost that battle!
I left to hide myself at the bottom of the bottle.

Lost.
!!2 YEARS!!
Lost.

I picked myself up.
I couldn't make you take my helping hand.
I left to try better my life.
Certified to save lives, but I couldn't save a single one.

You had to be the parent whilst I was gone.
Dinner. Red and white. 3rd time. Come home.
Mom needs you, we need you. Help.
That never should have been your role.

I failed you as a sister.

I couldn't make you feel loved enough.
I couldn't keep you safe.
I couldn't protect you.
I couldn't make you see your worth.
I couldn't help you see your potential.
And boy you had so much.
I couldn't keep you from the drugs.
I couldn't keep you from the thrill of that life.
I just couldn't keep you under my wing.
I left my youth lying with you on that computer room floor.
I let you down on one of my final missions for you.
I failed with your eulogy, you deserved so much more.

!!!!!!!!!!!!!I'M SORRY!!!!!!!!!!!!!

You and I were the best with our words.
I can't get my head on straight.
I can't find my legs. I keep staggering.
I can't hold anything, it keeps slipping, my fingers are numb.
I can't speak without biting my tongue.
I can't find my feelings.
I can't find my heart.
And ohh my soul.
It hurts soo.

stop.
..
Stop
...
Please Stop.
....
STOP!
.....
I think I found them.
......
Worse, they found me.
....

BROKENsoulBROKENheartBROKENmind

....

?feelings?

....

NOSTOP!!!

....

angerdenialsadinconsolablewoefulbluebad
depressedsorrowjoylessanguishedweeping

....

Slow down, not all at once.

....

I can't handle that much.

....

System overload.

....

ALEX.se.axe.ALEX.bde.hbf.ALEX.ase.soj.ALEX
ALEX.fc.bs.ALEX.jn.mj.ALEX.bbf.wb.lbf.ALEX

....

LOWenergystrengthfaithmotivationhope

....

BATTERYSHUTTINGDOWN

....

FAILURE

....

REBOOTING

....

My baby brother, I miss you so.
I'm sorry I failed you.
For this I can't seem to let you go.
How can I become worthy of your forgiveness?

HAPPY BIRTHDAY BABY AL,

Today is the day all of our lives changed
Today you would have been 24
Today would have been one of the happiest days

I hope your happy
I hope your healthy
I hope your smile is lighting up the heavens

I hope your with mom
I hope your with dad
I hope your with our brother
I hope your with our sister
I hope your with all our cousins
I hope your with the kids
I hope your with all our deadly aunties
I hope your whooping it up with the uncc's
I hope your with our grandfathers
I hope your with our grandmothers

I hope you know just how much I love you
I hope you know how much I miss you
I hope that your happy
I hope your healthy
I hope that your loved

That's the only thing that makes this easier
To hope

To hope I'll get to see you one day again
To hope for that day your laughter and voice is real
To hope for that day I don't have to close my eyes listening to your video loop
To hope for that day I won't have to pretend your here sitting with me in my war pony

NÍNEM

To hope for that day I can embrace you in a hug again

I hope you have everything you need in the heavens
I hope they answer your every desire
I hope they treat you like their own little brother
I hope you can feel my love from down here
I hope you know I speak of you often
I hope you know your missed beyond anything I could possibly write up in words
I hope you know I try my best
I hope you know you live on
I hope your happy
I hope your loved
I hope
I hope
I hope
I hope

CERTIFICATE

One certificate I wish I didn't hold
Two certificates I wish I didn't hold
I know my mothers gone
I know my brothers gone

Certificate of death
Only the [64]séme7 would need a silly paper
To tell them a loved ones passed on
Gone to the sky world

Lived to see their last sunrise
Lived to see their last sunset
Called home to the spirit world
Back to our [65]teqwétsten/[66]iihtsíístapipaitapiiyo'p

Back to [67]Apistotoke/[68]Tqeltkúkwpi7
I often wonder if you watched
Grandfather sun
Grandmother moon
On that dreaded day
Just like we used to

Whilst having a smoke
Or going for a drive
How can holding one paper
Cause me to go through so many feelings?

Too many in a short time
I'm left here a wreck
Staring aimlessly at this
Certified piece of paper

NÍNEM

Maybe if I stare long enough
It will disappear
And my brother could be here
This paper

Death certificate
Needed to grab a piece of your mail
Who would possibly of sent it
2020

A year that broke me
2023
What could it be?
Feeling like old times

When I got to take care of you
Being mad at myself
For all the times
I couldn't help you

What I wouldn't do to hear you say
Sister
[69]Kic, taxi me to town
[70]Ní'ssa make me my appointment
Sister take me to my appointment
Kic
Ní'ssa
Sister
How I wish I could hear that word
It's means nothing
Like this certificate of death
Sister
Just an empty word
Without you here

ON THOSE DAYS

On those days where you can't get out of bed
On those days where you wake up late
On those days where your body
Your spirit needed more rest
On those days where it takes fifteen minutes of lying there racking up the courage to put on your warrior face to battle the day that lies ahead
On those days where there is anger so deep you can feel it clench in your heart
On those days the anger radiates out to those around you
On those days where anger is really grief and the day is dragging on
On those days where you have faced every emotion and cried several times
On those days when you check the clock 11:31
How can it not even be noon yet?
On those days where nothing helps

Not feeling it
Not letting it flow
Not talking about
Not smudging
Not praying
Not yelling it out
Not crying it out
Not even the meds seem to be working today

On those days where the voice in your head send nothing but intrusive thoughts
On those days where those thoughts continuously bombard your brain
On those days where worries are extra strong
On those days where the past seems to much, the present

overwhelming, the future not enough
On those days usually mother nature calls out
My only true mother I have left in this realm
Today one of those days, it did
Mother Nature called out

Despite the black clouds approaching
Slowly encroaching our valley
Sleeking over the mountains
Like we couldn't hear its thunderous roars approaching

The tears here they come again
That anger boiling under my skin
Pleading me to punch anything
Within reach
Like the 2013 me

Looking over at the closest thing
A tree
In my head I know it physically won't get hurt
A tree
A youngin'
Stronger than me
Solid unlike me
It would bust up my bodies weak fragile hand

My soul knowing
Hurt would fall on this trees spirit, if I punched it
Thinking of all the different ways this
Little young tree has already helped me

Giving me life
Giving me nothing but love with every breath I take
Giving me a nice shady spot beneath its leafy green branches
Giving me a comfy resting spot when grandfather sun is beating down too hard

Helping me to proudly present some of my beaded creations

Helping me showcase them to the world
Helping me hold up passed on knowledge
Helping me pass on that knowledge for generations to come

Knowing I have grown
Just like this tree
That is rooted
Before me

Remembering when my family planted this tree
Back then when it was
Just a little baby
Barely reaching to my childish knee

Knowing I can't and won't harm this tree
One medium sized tree
That now looms
Over me

One coniferous tree that contributes to the forest that surrounds me
The forest
One small part that makes mother nature's heart beat
Mother nature she's calling to me

The tears, grief, anger
Consumes me all over again
Looking down at my moccasins
The tears race down my face and fall upon them

I know they won't do for this adventure
The one that lies ahead of me today
Going inside and switching them for gum boots
Not being able to remember the last time I put on [71]séme7e/[72] náápiikoan shoes

The soles feeling too thick under my feet
Walking down the familiar ground

Trying to hold it together
Trying not to make a crying sound as I trudge passed other humans
They're too far to see the tears streaming

The last thing I need today is more human beings
Still not even noon
11:48
Humans are the worst in the world

Getting to the right spot
The picnic table
Nestled under
A big leafy tree
Number [73]kellés/[74]nioókska

The forest to my right
My families potato patch to my left
Taking a seat it's so hard to catch my breath
Letting it all come out whilst I finish my smoke

Feeling the rain in the air
Smelling the familiar
Sweet scent of the forest
Buckie, birch, willow, wild rose, and rain fill the humid air

Nowhere else in the world has the same fragrance
This beautiful forest
Along the borders of my families lands
Gifted to us to care for, long before the settlers "explored" these lands

Walking along the edge
Until I see a thin enough opening
Time to go adventuring
[75]Skoden

In the heart of the forest

Once inside, I hear the robins
A crow laughs
A magpie lets out a startled cry
The raven calls out
Shaming me for scaring the poor little chickadee
Out of her home in the red willow

Sorry I didn't realize that tree was occupied
I just held on
I didn't want to fall
On the unstable ground
Us dang humans we're the worst

Fighting my way through the thick under bush
How our old childhood paths
Have overgrown
Thinking of the times that seem so long ago
Distant memories of happy times

Brothers
Sister
Cousins
Mother
Father
Uncles
Aunties
Grandmothers
Grandfathers
All still here on earth's side

All the times we went on adventures through this very bush
Entertaining ourselves all day
We made this place our own little city
Carving out walkways

Making this place into our own little map
One we would never forget

Yet years later
It looks like we were never here

The forest it grew
As the time went on
Flourishing
Without the little human beings rummaging inside

The tears start flowing again…
Ohh how beautiful heaven must be
Now you've all been called home
Your spirits filling that place with laughter and love
I know we will meet again
Some days the betrayal and hurt are just too much to hold

I'm stuck

I've hit a thick wall of underbrush
Rose thorns
And willows intertwined
Getting angry again

Knowing that there would have been easier paths
Help
Many years ago
Turning around

Thinking of giving up and going home
I've seen I'm too far in
Wanting to sit down in sorrow and self pity
But there's too many mosquitoes around

Mosquitoes the only thing
That gets excited when humans are around
They are flocking to see me
Surprised to see a human
All of them shouting eeee in my ear

Anger fueling me

To pursue
And find another way around
Not wanting to become a mosquito's smorgasbord

Spotting a fallen pine tree
This will require a fine balancing act
A new path meant for me to carve
It's leading me straight like I wanted

The undergrowth over growing this dead tree is thick
The new young trees using it as a stepping stone to grow
The old tree giving the required support
Even dead it's helping nurture the future generations

Having to still fight my way through
At least there's no thorns
Way up here
Using the last of the anger to push through the strong bendy red willows
Blocking my path
Breaking through everything that was holding me back
I made it to the end of the fallen tree
Looking at the stump that once held this old tree down
Seeing it gave way near the bottom
Snapped
Leaving its roots in the ground

Hearing the creek's beautiful sound
The work I put in
Worth it
I see the flowing water now

Walking up the creek
Letting all my tears fall
To be swept away into the
Little currents below

Walking up the creek

NÍNEM

Knowing the water that flows around me is life
Its sacred
It will never be in the same place twice

I weave my way through the creek bed
Until I'm at the familiar spot
A miniature waterfall
Rubber boots what a wonderful thing I think to myself now

A water journey
So much easier then
Having my boots
On the ground

I stop and sing it out
Missing you
Northern Cree
Knowing I'm safe to sing along in this hidden spot

Feeling lighter
After letting it out
Letting it flow
Like the creek moving around me

The thunder shakes the forest around
The birds tell me
Change in weather is coming
I don't want to leave
I keep walking up the creek
Taking my time
In awe of the beauty around me
The music of the forest
It's beautiful
Especially backed by the
The bass of the booming thunder

Stopping to take pictures now
My spirit rejuvenated

Wanting to remember this memory
The magic gifted today

Human error
My phone dips into the creek
Good thing they're semi water proof
I'm not even mad over such a mundane thing, right now

FIGHTING THE COLD

I'm done fighting the cold
Time to embrace it.
Laydown in it
Let its powers do its work
It burns as I feel its fingers crawling up my skin
I think that's as bad as it gets
Just as I feel a stab in the back
I go to turn around
And get blown to the ground
I turn to face my enemy
There is nothing there
Just the wind
I realize it's just me!
I'm going crazy
Maybe it's just this cold
Chattering through my teeth
I'm so confused
Why I am going in circles
I'll just lay here
Until I go purple
Then blue
Let the cold take over
Let it numb me
If it's kind enough maybe it'll freeze me

HASTINGS SHUFFLE

We came from downstairs
You up stairs
[76]Slé7e and I stopping
In our tracks
Watching you do the funky chicken
The Hastings shuffle
Shaking our heads in unison
You looking at Slé7e
Knowing you lost control
Saying you shouldn't be awake
Him giggling
You looking to me, eyes pleading
Please don't say anything
Even though you know he knows
Your home
Your trying
To keep that promise
To the great grandparents
This is breaking me
Even more
Than
Your actions
Baby Al's actions
This is the worst part
Watching others struggle
Watching you
Harm others
You watching yourself
Harm others
Knowing
Their hearts
Are breaking

DAMN GOLF CART

Today realizing that another
Trauma filled cycle
Has been completed
Once again

You'd think it would get easier
You'd get used to the merry-go-round
That the feelings would just go more numb
The more you got pushed around and around

Wrong!
Same track
Stuck at the same spot
Spinning the same loop

New things getting thrown at the loop
Being pushed faster than ever before
Stopped!!!!
Never knowing when you'll be pushed around again

And again
And again
And again
And again

Last nights a little worse
He was high outta his mind
Many times
My "Brother"

Has tried to stand toe to toe
Always being the referee
Between him
And my late Brother

Alex
Alex Xavier Eugene
How I miss you
It's soul shattering in so many different ways

Your own brother
Your twin
The main reason your laying
6 feet underground

Even reading your name as I type it brings
Instant tears to my eyes
Having to hold them back
For what seems the zillionth time

Feeling my heart break over and over again
That clenching feeling around my heart
Radiating down my arm
To familiar of a feeling now

I can't help but think of all the times
You two went toe to toe
Him always grabbing the weapon first
He's so lost inside, anger is all he's known

Remembering that time
He had you holed up under the crib with a big butcher knife
Or that time he beat you with a pipe
Or that time he maced you in the grandparent's basement

I refuse to continue being one of his victims
I've been pushed around enough
He's pushed others around enough
It will end with me

Go ahead
Take it out on me

NÍNEM

Thankful last night I went out
Instead of our great grandparents

At least that's what I tell myself
To try make myself feel better
Knowing it's the truth but it rips me apart inside
Sometimes doing the right thing isn't as easy as it seems

But would I change a thing?
This cycle is gonna end
You will understand that there are consequences
To your actions

Last night broke my heart
My soul
Two of the same
Two

Two
Twins
Birthday soon
He's hurting too

He's hurting
Has been since young
Broken
All of us on the [77]rez are

We are all healing in our own ways, just trying to find that love and understanding
Last night a test to see how far I've come
Not stopping
To continue engaging

These drugs
Take away people's respect
For themselves
And others too

So unpredictable
How are they riding the high?
How'd they take that last hit?
Is it a good trip or a bad one

Yesterday high all day
Nodding off on [78]Kyé7e's couch
You could barely stand
And pour yourself a bowl of cereal

All day my emotions festering and boiling
Ripping me apart inside
How can I feel this way to a "Brother"
With his actions was he ever a real one?

Raping young girls
Since too young of an age
An endless battle
Fighting others to just do the right thing!!

Nooo help
In that regard
Not the first time
I've been let down

Failed by the police
By the courts
Adults
Family
The band
The whole system
How do you keep giving him bail!

Last night the old me
Really wanting to step through
To stop and engage in the endless cycle
To convert my NRG to hate and rage

Fighting something that will never change
You think you can get angry and let your traumas
Project on to me
Boy you don't know what I've been through

Almost letting the old Harriet
Shine on through
What was going through
Your mind

Trying to block the door from me to bring
Those effen cart keys in
The ones you were joy riding on
2300 hundred [79]slé7e just spent to fix the thing

Found you digging in his shop
Looking for who knows what
Finding today you stole 2 more jerry cans of diesel, 2 batteries
Who knows what else too

The old me would have been raging
The moment I saw you pull that camper in
More untrustworthy
Unpredictable people

That driver you chose
Pulling a long fifth wheel
Into the grandparents R.V. park
Looks just as high as you!

You'd thinking you would have learnt what harm
Driving high
Could do, the hurt it brings
After we lost mom
So many families/communities hurt

Choosing not to waste that energy
Choosing to look the other way

Until I saw you joy riding
On that damn cart

Knowing Slé7e
Has been at his wits end
Feeling the hurt radiate within him
As the bills of things you steal and break keeps rising

Those tools
Gas
Carts
Parts
Tools
Safe
Money
Gun
The list could go on

That's how Slé7e has made his living for
Our family
He's worked so hard for everything
Yet all you do is steal it from this 87 year old man

So I chose then when I saw you joy riding on that cart and digging through his gas shed
That I had to stand up
And go bring those damn cart keys

The old me wanting to let all my anger at you out right off the bat
To scream and shout
And cuss you out

Instead I walked over
Calm at first I said
What the hell do you think you're doing?
Show some respect to the old man

You know how much he spent to fix this damn cart

You know he's told you to stay the hell out of his shops
Get out, sober up
And leave the damn cart
I'll put it on the charger and take the keys in

You started to scream and yell
Saying you weren't high
Oh how I've heard that lie
A million times

You trying to stand up to me
Blocking the way to the cart
Trying to intimidate me
Then running to it as I try just to walk around

Barley avoiding knocking me to the ground
Another of your intimidation tactics
I've unfortunately learnt throughout the years
Flooring it in reverse almost running over me and skidding to the charging station

Telling you to go to sleep
To go and sober up
Stepping in to grab the keys
As your yelling guhh tell me I'm not sober

Even though your eyes
Say different
No pupils in the night
Your jaws just a-going

Your legs can barely hold you up
Holahh boy stager straight
Trying to run into the house
To take cover under [80]Kyé7e's wing

I was just trying to go inside to bring those cart keys in
The front door locked

You turning around abruptly
Spitting your words in my face

Yelling around
Guhh let's sort this out now
Since your following me around
Saying let's talk this out as your fist are clenched at your sides

I told you already I'm just trying to bring these effen cart keys in
Parts of the old me slip out
Leave me alone you effen junky

Go to your trailer and sleep this s**t out
Eff off already I shout over the profanities he's spitting out
I see I made it worse
Turning around to leave
To try get in the back door

Feeling like I wanna angry cry
Feeling like I wanna shut down
The doctors words
PTSD kick in

Fight or flight
Fight or flight
I've fought to long, I don't know how much I got left in me
Flight

I won't freeze here
Trying to get off the deck even faster
The as****le runs through me to get to the stairs
My back was turned
Luckily I caught my feet

I'm still standing my ground
You blocking the stairs and ramp
My only way out
You b***h we're going to finish this now

Freeze
Assessing
Fight or flight
No way out

Flight, assessing
Flight it will have to be
No one has obviously heard the yelling around
Help won't come

Yelling are you serious you wanna try get tough
Let me through you damn junky
Start showing some respect
Stalking towards me

I pushed you away from me, buying a little time
The only way I could push was towards the stairs
I didn't give it all I had knowing just how high you were
Running back to the front door hoping it really wasn't locked
Hoping you told one of your famous lies, just so I would not get in

I think it was then
When I turned around
Locked out
Locked on the deck
I think it was then
My fight kicked in
No other choice
My back to a wall

I looked you square in the eye
As you were calling me c**t for trying to push you down the stairs
Even though you only really staggered down 3 of the stairs
If only this was 7 years back

I woulda gladly let all my anger, pain and trauma caused by you out
How it was tempting to sucker punch you in the face
Yelling now as your coming towards me

Harriet Samsquatch, my otherside coming out
The fighter
Brother to Brother
I puffed my chest out

Saying go ahead try me
I'm done trying to be nice now
Get out of my way let me out
Or you'll find out what will happen

His turn to be frozen
Maybe realizing how high he is
Before he could say two words
I started making fast heavy strides
Get walking or I'll really push you down these stairs

Reluctantly he starts staggering down them
Stopping at the ground turning around
Ready to fight
Speed walking to the back door

My dogs been going crazy
She hears him yelling around
I pray
Please don't let her barking wake my boy

He doesn't need to see this going down
This lifestyle
This type of trauma I've been trying to protect him from
Please let him sleep peacefully through this

Great he's following me now
Running the last few steps to the back door

Creating a little space
One prayer heard this one's open, locking it behind me

Kyé7e's been awake this whole time sitting on the couch
No hearing aids in
Not a damn clue to what just happened

Trying to quickly explain
Leaving the keys
Saying I'm done with this I need to go and check on my boy
He's really high out of his mind tonight

Braving myself for the 200 meter walk home
No way I can get there without
"The little brother" seeing
Knowing he's had enough time to maybe find a weapon
Knowing all he knows is anger
He's in is element
Knowing there's a 50/50 chance
I'll be chased with a weapon

Sure enough
As soon as he hears my steps
I barely made it to the apple tree
He emerged yelling from the dark

I can barely see him in the shadows
Yelling your just a w***e
You think your tough now
I'm broken, I'm hurt, I'm tired

Flight is upon me
I just want to be in my home
Safe
Guarding my little boy

Yelling
Keep it up

Come close to me or my house
I'll call the cops, they might take awhile

But come close to me I'll run to my door
Karma will come out, she can do her job
She will protect me
It's what's [81]sqéxe/[82]nitómitaama instincts do

Go to sleep
Sober up
Leave me be
I got to the house

Made it inside
My boy he's still sleeping
My second prayer heard
To scared to go out for a smoke to calm my nerves
Sitting on my couch replaying the things that just happened
Not even [83]mus/[84]nissó minutes
He's already back digging in Slé7e's shed

Running with hands full up to that camper
To far away to see
What exactly it is
Knowing I have to go back over

I didn't mention the trailer
It slipped my mind
I didn't see him come back down
He started screaming and yelling again

Thankful this time
I leashed my protector
Brought her with me
She started her barking immediately

He didn't dare take any steps towards me
He froze then started yelling oh now you brought your dog

Good [85]sqéxe/[86]imitáá watch him
Keep him away from me

Rushing into the house before his fight kicked in
Telling Kyé7e about that fifth wheel
And all the things being brought up there from the shop
Saying just let me call the cops

Kyé7e
Not wanting to
Saying let me go wake Slé7e, see what he thinks
I tell Slé7e everything
Including the stairs

The reason I have my dog too
She's unhappy when Slé7e says he just wants to call the cops, too

Kye7e trying to send Slé7e out to take care of things
Me saying Sle7e please don't
It's dark, they are so unpredictable with how high they are
He's even coming after me right now
He's high he's not stable now

[87]Kyé7e won't stop saying talk to them first, enabling his behavior
Instilling its okay for him to lie, cheat, and steal
Don't call the cops
Me standing up saying fine I'll go
Don't send Slé7e out
He has half an hour to get that camper off the property

Walking up with my protector [88]nsqéxe/[89]nitómitaama
Up to two drug ridden people
The owner trying to lie
Not knowing I watched my "Brother" jump out of his truck
Not knowing I've been watching him run things up

He raises his voice

Not wanting to leave
Saying he won't
He looks just as high as my "brother"

I shine my light on the truck getting a look at the silver color
Red fx on the side
Major damage to the backend
Bed of the truck filled with many wires
Saying the owners want you off the property
You have half an hour before the cops are called
Knowing I would call them anyways, these guys are driving high!!

Going back down filling the grandparents in
He won't leave
Lying says he don't know him
Just gave him a ride

He didn't take anything he brought it
[90]Slé7e starts his truck
The guy he yells at him too
Twice now he's been asked to leave

Slé7e gets uncle
Things get heated between the camper
And him too
Third time

He says he won't leave
I call the cops dispatch
It's not until he hears I'm actually on the phone
He starts rushing to get his stuff ready to leave

He's gone before the cop on duty
Even calls me back
Giving the trucks description
I didn't even have to finish

Yup he's well known

NÍNEM

We know where to look
He's often parked on a Radium back road
Made the right judgment call
He's known to deal

SPERM DONOR

The dark wants to consume
Hysterical laughter
Tears running down my face
Shaking from anger

Feeling so helpless
Hurt
Seeing others hurt
Over and over

By you
One "man"
One "human being"
What did us children ever do to you?

When will it ever end
Just when I think there is light
That my trials are over
Boom

Another stab in the back
How many times am I supposed to rise from feeling this low?
This pain it's different
How could one "person"

Have so much resentment
Passing on so much pain over and over again
What did I ever do to deserve this kind of treatment from you?
My own blood "father"

A PICTURE WORTH 1000 WORDS

Found some old pictures
It's these little things
That matter
That I cherish

Good times with family
Over 15 years ago
A quick snapshot
A throwback Thursday

That brings me back
Into feels
Like it was only yesterday
Missing those times

Missing that home
Missing Mom
Missing Dad
Missing Big Ears and Baby Al
My two sweet brothers
Missing sister Bee
Missing Uncle Buffalo and Blair
Auntie Linda
Buster
Grandma Florence and
Too many others

Mans family
That adopted us
Babes
The twins
And me
As their own kin too

Seeing these reminded me of the first time I moved to Lil Chicago
A little girl
Fresh out of grade [91]seséle/[92]naato'ka
Standing on those front steps
For the first time
Glaring down that front door
Like a little witch

Unsure what I should do
So there I stood
Outside that little blue house
That would soon become my home

Scared
Nervous
Taken out of music class
Mom
Stealing
Her children back

No goodbyes
To the grandparents
Or other family members
Before I crossed those mountains

My first war pony ride with Henry
Mom driving
He's riding shotgun
A twin, a brother on either side

Laughter, smiles
Love
Mother and daughter reunited
New family in creation

Goodbye what a silly word
For it's never goodbye

It's [93]Kitatama'sino/[94]me7 wíktsen
Something I had yet to learn

The beginning of beginnings
Turning this bush NDN
Into a prairie NDN
Hillbilly to the bone

Seeing that lamp post
Brought tears to my eyes
Thinking of that one time
I walked back from the community center

Remembering my brother
The clock tower
Laying there
Passed out

He left from the stick game
Our team kept loosing
I had a feeling, other then frustration
I went home to check things out

There he was
Hugging that lamp post
Passed out
He was a heavy sleeper

Once he was out
He was out
No one else was home
No cell phones back then

Couldn't call
Or text
My three other brothers
For backup then

I knew he was breathing

Scared
I checked
For the rise and fall

My brother he was tall
I was just the little sister
I couldn't
Wouldn't leave him

Sleeping
Vulnerable
Under that lamp post
So I dragged him

Hoping he would wake up
I grabbed him under the arms
He didn't, so I dragged him
Across the little parking lot

My brother was a giant
6ft tall
A warrior
With a heart of gold

Oh how funny
This must of looked
It's a good thing
We were on the rez

Because this is something
That the [95]séme7/[96]náápiikoan
Just wouldn't understand
It's the outcome of residential "schools"

We made it across
The parking lot
Now
Those [97]teq'mékst/[98]Naoi stairs

Looked like a mountain
I pulled him up the first three
Then the invisible man
Pulled him to the bottom

He didn't fall down gracefully
He awoke
When he hit the concrete
At the bottom

Looking around he was ready to fight
It musta felt like he got kicked in the ass
I couldn't stop laughing
He didn't believe

He didn't remember
Falling asleep
Under that lamp post
No way you dragged me

Your too small
I showed him the drag marks
Then we tried to go in
But the front door was locked

There was a deep freeze
Blocking the back door
So he lifted me up
On his shoulders

And I climbed in the kitchen window
My very first B & E
I used the ledge of those front steps
To help balance myself out

These pictures
Have turned into a thousand words
My mind won't stop running

Finally unlocked priceless memories

That my mind
My body
Had tucked
Away

Remembering when we used to live
In the other house in the picture
For a short while
Whilst ours was being fixed
After the first small flood

I remember when that guy
Tried to steal my brand new bike
From mom and dad
He tried to take the path

He shouldn't have tried to take a short cut
He didn't expect the dip
The front wheel hit hard
He flew over the handlebars

There we were
The twins
Andrew
Me

Laughing hysterically
We went to go check it out
The guy knocked himself out
He lost his left shoe

Andrew grabbed my bike
Off the guy
Al grabbed a stick and poked him
He didn't move

All of a sudden

He shot up
And raced away like a hare
We spent the rest of the day

Playing in the trees
High up off the ground
You see in the pictures
I remember the fun had on the rope swing

Watching our bikes
Like a [99]tsícwts'ecw
Until Mom, Dad, and Grandma Florence
Came back from the casino in the city

Now I remember
Now I know
Why they say a picture is worth a thousand words
Today I was brought back in time

Today I was given the gift of a few memories
It felt like I was there again with my family
All from a simple lost picture
A priceless artifact to me

To my family
My ancestors above
[100]Yerí7 skukwstsétsemc for this gift today
I hope you guys are happy,together and whole
I hope you guys crossed over easily
I hope all you know is light and love
For the heavens better know just what they have

MOVED BACK HOME

Looking forward to the release
Stretching and pushing
Looking after my physical shell

Got addicted to the pain
The gym my only release
Maybe that's why I thought I was happy
So many moons ago

I moved back to the small town
The one that used to provide
Safety, comfort, shelter, food, prosperity, hope, unity and life

I moved back to the small town
The one that I thought I never could
Too much: pain, hurt, memories, deaths, failed dreams, dreams left to die, dreams left to come true, stolen innocence, broken promises, greed… too much for one life

I moved back to that small town
A calling I could always feel in my bones
To the land
To the beautiful creation

Things shut down
Gym's schedule never matched up

No way to deal with it
No way to self inflict the pain
Hurt with nowhere to go
You see pain's how I've been known to be living

One death after another

Theirs:Mine:Theirs:Mine:Theirs:Mine:
Theirs:Mine:Theirs:Mine:Theirs:Mine:
Theirs:Mine:Theirs:Mine:Theirs:Mine:
Theirs:Mine:Theirs:Mine:Theirs:Mine:
Theirs:Mine:Theirs:Mine:Theirs:Mine:
Theirs:Mine:Theirs:Mine:Theirs:Mine:

But they say mine will always be last
For some say 2 spirits are destined
Destined to live
Gifted chances to get to know and relive in this ever changing world

Forever given the gift to see the good, the bad and the ugly
In each and every lifetime
Witnessing the beauty, simplicity, excitement, silly, crazy, and impossible
Moving, living and adapting with all parts of creation

Just living
Slowly releasing, stretching and pushing
Through it all
The good, the bad, and the ugly

I moved back to that small town.
That one that I thought of as a mere graveyard

That small town slowed things
Made things timeless, as it should be
No clock towers dwelling over you
Getting lost in the magic

I moved back to the small town.
My now creation of home.
My homeland passed on to me from my [101]teqwétsten/[102]iihtsíístapipaitapiiyo'p
Taken care of by my family/nation

Gifted to us since the beginning of our time of creation
To love, protect, and cherish
So we all may marvel at the beauty of it for many moons to come
So I moved back home
For these lands they call to me

I moved back home to that little town
I moved back home to the lands
I moved back home to the people
I moved back home to the magic
I moved back home to wonder
I moved back home to the spirits.

I wanna say I moved back home to the spot of creation

For my eyes have seen it
In the mountains, animals, trees, rivers, and humans
I have seen it in the spirits that choose to stay
Those that choose to come back home

I stretched and pushed my pain back into creation
Having faith creator heard my prayer
To not harm anyone or anything with it
For I know in this life what's enough pain to be worse than a forbidden curse

Washed away, taken to the darkness, stripped naked to my flesh

My fears…
Trusting and femininity right there
Giving myself back to creation
To the glacial water

Body
Mind
Spirit
Freezing, slowing, numbing, freezing, stopping

Hoping, knowing I'll be gifted with another chance
To be humbled for that breath of air

Or…

Will I finally be free
Deemed worthy enough after giving my being over and over again
This "or" seems impossible for us 2 spirits
For we are destined
[103]2S
Forever protectors of creation
2S
Forever protectors of each other

I heard you say, open your eyes my child
I did
Finally giving my all to you
My eyeballs freezing

Vision straining
Looking into the dark frigid waters
Looking into you
I thought I was going to seize…

You caught me again though
Renewing my trust in our little game
Stretching our bond a little further
You pushed me to the surface

Allowing me to suck in that piercing cold air
Allowing it to warm my lungs
It's been 2 days since I really moved back home

The new and the old
The past selves are forgotten to time
Now colliding with the new

Finding harmony from how it used to be
Adapting to how it is now must be
It's been 12 hrs since I realized
...

..

.

I'm home
I'm back
.

..

..

...

I had to run to one of my Mommas
Releasing and stretching out to her
Another old familiar soul that chooses to stay
In this small town, that I just couldn't see before

Running into her arms in this life
Even if she doesn't see it yet
Trusting
I see the parts that do
Saying Momma I'm home

Being asked " Well where have you been?"
Well Momma I've been in the far and the between
Sometimes stuck or going too fast
Sometimes I've been stuck looking at the ugly
Sometimes I was lost to Time himself
Sometimes I couldn't bare to look at myself
But Momma I'm home now, thank you

Tonight I'm looking forward to the release, stretching, and pushing

NÍNEM

Looking after the physical shell
For I fell in love with yoga
For I fell in love with gym

Bringing balance to the pain
Looking after more than just my physical shell, but my soul at the same time
For I have truly come back home
Forever releasing, stretching, and pushing
To be worthy of when it's my soul's final time

A GREAT GIFT

A great gift left to me
Unexpectedly
A gift I would give up
If it meant still having you here
I can't comprehend

Why
Why, why I keep asking
A gift that would change my life, my son's
How many more generations down my line

It would be a nice break
Like the ones we would take
When I lived with you
Watching your house for 10 months

I miss our conversations
Our breaks
Endless learning
About
Each other

Grandfather
Granddaughter
Old
New

You growing up strong
Seeing me growing up strong
You turning into a businessman
Passing tips for my small business

Through your stories
Your life's lessons
To anyone

NÍNEM

Willing to listen

You listening to mine
Learning
About
The NDN ways

You surprised
I knew
So much
Of your god

In the end I knew
You knew
As much about
[104]Apistotoke/[105]Tqeltkúkwpi7

Hearing
This Tiggers
Lost his bounce
Laying Baby Al down to rest

Then Uncc
Your beautiful baby boy
[106]Kellés/[107]nióókska funerals together, in such a short time
Having you as my support

Knowing I didn't have to worry
With you there behind me
Through so many other
Funerals

Grandparents
Great grandparents
Me
Making funeral preparations

No mom
No dad

No parents
This isn't the way it should be

You seeing the coffin
That I signed off on
Saying that's not nice enough
For my grandson

Tears
Shakily, pointing to one
Saying I/we can't afford it
The band only helps cover so much
This is good, we'd be happy in just a plain box

It's how we were raised
Even this one here
He'd say it's deadly
The look on his face

The NDNs
And him
Bust out laughing
We all got laughter is medicine in dark times

He pointed to a coffin
Creator blue
With chrome
The finest wood
Worth more than he
Than I had ever seen

That one's good enough
For my grandson
Me letting you choose
Letting you do what you feel you need to

To help send him off on his final journey
His journey back home

NÍNEM

To Apistotoke/Tqeltkúkwpi7
To god

Surprised
Those DVD
God sermons
Like the ones on Sunday mornings

When we only had the black and white
Bunny eared T.V.
We're the only thing that calmed him down
In the end

Second time signing those funeral papers
Over ten grand
For simple funerals
We go to Shuswap Cemetery

No additional burial plot fees
Embalming
Weekend fees
You have to do your own obituary cards
It's to short notice for the weekend

So soon
After our mother's
No blood father insight
You bringing him up

A known sore subject
You called and told him
He yelled at you for being a grandfather
Inviting us to family functions
Having us for Christmas and summer break

He always blames everyone else for his problems
I see the heartbreak
In your eyes

The heartbreak in mine
When I said I know

He dodged my calls
I even tried to let him know about our mother
He dodged my calls
About Alex too

You knowing how we grew up on the [108]rez
We talked about it
Over dinner
Over too lemony, lemon pie

Welfare to welfare check
On the rez
Picking bottles
Picking mint and various berries

Making money from nothing
But what others throw away
And what creation
Has to offer

I wonder if you saw
I wasn't raised
The twins
Weren't raised

How we could have been
But as rough as it was
I still came out
A good hearted person

Even though at times I don't remember it
I remember getting out of the physic ward
You were the first call
You asked me to come live with you

Promising things would be so different

NÍNEM

Oh how I wish I could have
I should have said
Yes

But I wouldn't leave my
Brothers
My sisters
My culture

We were often left alone
Kids watching kids
Learning
When to stand up for ourselves

Too young
Fighting
The NDNs
The anger, hate, abuse

Passed on from nuns and priests
Fighting intergenerational trauma
Fighting family
Fighting the [109]séme7/[110]náápiikoan
Fighting the government

Me wondering if you saw
If you heard
You listened
You remembered

Our stories
Our mothers stories
Our [111]Kyé7e stories
Our [112]Slé7e stories

Is this why
You left such an extravagant
Unexpected gift to me

A way to still take care of us

Forgotten
[113]Sq'wtew's/[114]aanáokitapiikoan
Children
Grandchildren
To the séme7/náápiikoan side

They were never there
Even when we were just down the road
I was in grief
A single mother
Mourning her mother

An old life
The old ones never reaching out
Unless your were persistent with them
Making it feel forced

Maybe they were to scared
Scared of us savages
Sq'wtew's/aanáokitapiikoan
I wonder what stories the sperm donor might have told them

He's never been all there
Something grandpa and I talked of often
He always blamed himself for his children's failures
There were many he'd say

I'd always say
Grandpa it's not your fault
You gave them everything and more
The choices they make as adults
Are not yours to carry

You always saw us as family
Those that shared your house
Saw us as family too

NÍNEM

Nieces, nephews, grandkids, great grandkids

They, you were family
You always had you door open
Just like us NDNs
You took care of your blood kin

Just like us NDNs
You choose to see the similarities
Just like us NDNs
You chose love

Just like us NDNs
Something
I feel is lost
To those fighting against your final wishes

Your own children
My own "father"
Old aunts
Old uncles

Fighting
Greed
Power
Taking over their hearts

Did they ever hear
Did they ever listen
Did they ever watch
Did they ever learn

All that you
Grandpa Tigger
Had to offer
They could have learnt so much

Life skills

The seme7/náápiikoan way
The bush way
The NDN way
How to be giving

How to be helpful
How to see others as human beings
How to say your piece
And forgive

Maybe then they wouldn't be fooled by this law firm
Who goes along with whatever
Nonsense
They don't seem reputable to me
What do they care
They are going to retire from this

Why go along with grandpas wishes
Your paying their bills now
I thought they were supposed to protect us
Not change this and take away from his grandchildren and great grandchildren

Where is their love?
Grandpa shouldn't have been to scared in the end
To change things
Or they'd fight
His own children
That he wasn't in the right mind

Where is their respect
To honor your wishes
Your late son
Your widow
Your baby girl
Your grandchildren
Your great grandchildren

Themselves?
Where is the honor to you?

As your faith
As your last wishes
Showed just how much
You had for each of us

WANT TO MAKE IT A COMPETITION

You told me today to be thankful I have my son
I am everyday
I've lost two children before
That s**ts painful
D and C
I faced it all alone
You were surrounded by family

I just got a lecture and hurtful words from your mother
You said I'm lucky
You don't have a kid anymore
I know that loss
I just stayed quiet

You said I had a son so I had someone
You said you had no one
But you do
I stayed quiet, for it's not a competition

Not my place to compare our traumas
Your child
Lived with me under my roof for years
We lived under my parents roof together for years
Your child was my sister
I recognize your hurt
I lost her too
Multiple times
Over
And over again to the addiction
Just like my mother
Just like my father

Just like my 3 brothers
Just like unc
I stayed quiet

You have your parents
I don't
You have your siblings
I don't
I stayed quiet

A moment of silence
Hearing you in the background
Waiting for your hurt to finish coming out in the wrong way
Thinking of
My two sweet angels above
Knowing they are safe and happy
With my family that has been called home
To [115]Apistotoke/[116]Tqeltkúkwpi7
Rest easy [117]teqwétsten/[118]iihtsíístapipaitapiiyo'p:
AXE
SFE
WBJ
ASE
HBF
AE
FE
BDE
DW
FBF
MJ
WBJ
EW
WW
SOJA
BBF
SD

LBF
TD
ML
FC
JN
BS
FB
CC
BM
DJ

BEAUTY IN DEATH

There is beauty in death
The weight being lifted
The possibility of the new unknown
Stopping after the grief consumes you

Looking at the world with new eyes
Looking at the mountains
Looking at the trees
The crisp untouched snow

Letting your inner child out again
Free to explore
Free to be vulnerable
Free to be trusting

Knowing safety
Knowing comfort
Knowing it's okay to sing to the world
Singing to old selves
Singing out the hurt
Singing and truly feeling all the emotions

Being new, but wise enough to acknowledge the old
Being new and curious
Still going fourth
Chasing that feeling of the beautiful unknown

SHELL OUT

Today I'm coming out of my shell
Crying
A picture speaks a thousand words
But clicked at the right moment it can trap beauty

It's in the eyes of the beholder
The feels in that moment
Feels that hurt so bad
I gotta wash them off

Crying alone in the shower
Feeling that hurt sink in
Tearing apart my heart and soul
So familiar

Clenching my fist
The old me showing through
Anger
Wanting to punch a hole in the wall

Letting out that pain, hurt and anguish
The pain radiating from my core down my arm
Crying
Riding the waves out

The highs
The lows
And the
Undertows

I had shut off joy
For it hurts
Know what it feels like
Having it taken in seconds

NÍNEM

Gone through it too many times
Too many times
Today I'm coming back out of my shell
I'm taking back my power

8 LONG YEARS

8 long years
Battles upon battles
That turned into wars
Endless fighting
Even the voices in my own head
Oh the trauma endured
Today preparing to enter the arena
One more time
War paint on
Heart armored
Just one more time
Feeling the finality of it
That victory finally within reach
Praying for that victory
Hopeful I can rest
Easily tonight
Take off my armor
And set it to the side
Whilst I sing my victory cry

GLOSSARY SECWÉPEMCTSÍN (SHUSWAP)

Secwépemctsín	Phonetic	English
Custwést	Kust-wust	Mischievous One
Kellés	Ka-glass	Three
Kenpésq't	Ken-pes-kt	Shuswap Band in Invermere B.C.
Kic	Kic	Older sister
Kí7ce	Gee7-kha	Mother
K̓wséltkten	Kwah-selt-kin	Family
Kyé7e	Key-ya7-ah	Grandmother
Me7 wíktsen	Ma7-week-chee	See you later
Mus	Moose	Four
Nínem	Nee-nem	Hoot of an owl
Peq[7]	Paq	White color
Secwépemctsín	Suh-kwep-mec-scheen	Language of the Shuswap
Séme7	Sam-mauh	Caucasian
Seséle	Se-sel-la	Two
Slé7e	Sla-uha	Grandfather

Sníne	Sne-ena	Owl
Sqéxe	Ska-ha	Dog
Sq'wteẃs	Sam-mauh-jeep	Half breed
Teqltkúkwpi7	T-quelt-kook-pi7	Creator
Teq'mékst	Tuk-mack-st	Six
Teqwétsten	Ts-cowl-wolth	Ancestors
Tsícwts'ecw	Ts-chee-qwelth	Fish Hawk
Tsútsllke7	Tsu-ch-ka	Seven
Weytk	Why-t-k	Hello
Yeri7 skukwstsétsemc	Yew-we-skoot-skat-chem	Thank you very much

GLOSSARY SIKSIKÁ (BLACKFOOT)

Siksiká	Phonetic	English
Aanáokitapíikoan	Aah-nok-gah-tap-pi-koan	Half breed
Áápi	Aa-pi	White color
Apistotoke	Ahp-iss-toh-toh-kee	Creator
Ihkitsik	Ick-git-sik-a	Seven
Iihtsíístapipaitapiiyo'p	Iss-tii-pay-to-pii-yohp	Ancestors
Imitáá	Ii-mi-ta	Dog
Kitatama'sino	Key-tat-ah-mah-say-no	See you later
Na'á	Na-ah	Addressing mother
Náápikoan	Naa-pi-koan	Caucasian
Naato'ka	Naa-too-ka	Two
Naoi	Noi	Six

Niksíssta	Ni-ksis-ta	My mother
Nioókska	Nee-ook-skaa	Three
Nískso'kowaiksi	Nii-sko-ko-walks	Family/Relative
Ni'ssa	Nin-ssta	Older sister (male perspective)
Nissó	Nee-si-woo	Four
Nitómitaama	Nii-to-mii-ta	My Dog
Oki	Oki	Hello
Siksiká	Sik-sik-a	Blackfoot people

GLOSSARY SLANG

Slang	Phonetic	English
Bepsi	bep-si	Pepsi
MMIW	MMIW	Murdered Missing Indigenous Women
NDN	N-D-N	Indian
Skoden	Sko-den	Let's go then
Rez	Rez	Reservation
2S	2S	Two spirit

ABOUT THE AUTHOR

Sasha Eugene

Sasha saw her first sunrise in Invermere, British Columbia. Her first gifted home was to the Sexwepmec'u'lecw. By blood she is Kinbasket, Secwepemc, and Russian. In the early 2000's she moved to her second gifted home in Siksika, Alberta. Sasha enjoys being out in creation with her seven year old son. They practice hunting, berry picking, gathering traditional medicine, dancing, and playing lahal. Growing up she was fortunate to have many teachers and supporters to help teach and guide her along the Red Road. Sasha is grateful to have the chance to learn and practice the language of her two homes, Secwépemctsín and Siksiká.

Manufactured by Amazon.ca
Bolton, ON